Marshmallows
and
Nougat

25 LIGHT AND FLUFFY GOURMET TREATS

CAROL PASTOR

LORENZ BOOKS

Contents

Introduction

At first glance, light and fluffy marshmallows and dense sticky nougats may seem daunting to make at home, but this book will reveal how to transform simple sugar syrups and fresh egg whites into various pretty and tasty treats. This chapter gives all the technical information every sweet-maker needs up his or her sleeve. You will find advice on equipment and ingredients plus step-by-step technique sequences to demonstrate the skills for mastering these irresistible confections.

Sweet, fluffy and lighter than air, marshmallows hold a special place in our childhood memories. Whether toasted over an open fire or dunked into piping hot chocolate, these simple gooey treats have been enjoyed by countless children and adults alike for more than a century.

A History of Marshmallows

EARLY HISTORY

Marshmallows take their name from the marshmallow plant, a wild herb with a fleshy stem and five petalled flowers which grows in marshland. It was used as early as 2000BC by the Ancient Egyptians for making sweets, boiling pieces of marshmallow root to extract the gelatinous sap and combining it with honey until it thickened. The mixture was strained and left to cool to create delicacies for the exclusive preserve of their Gods and nobility. The marshmallow plant continued to be used in the same process during the 14th and 15th centuries, but for medicinal purposes rather than confectionery.

EUROPEAN BEGINNINGS

It wasn't until 1850 that French candy makers produced marshmallows similar to how we know them today, using the mallow root sap as a binding agent and adding beaten egg whites, corn syrup and water, and occasionally rose water. The mixture was heated and poured into small individual cornstarch moulds (known as the starch mogul system), and was called *paté de guimauve*. The manufacturing process of marshmallows remained limited on a small, almost individual, scale until the mid twentieth century, when mass production became possible through the extrusion process. In extrusion the marshmallow mixture is pressed through tubes to form long continuous ropes of marshmallow, which are then cut into small equal pieces, tumbled in cornstarch to counter their stickiness, and left to dry. Gelatin gradually replaced the mallow root as a binding agent but the candy still kept its name.

Meert, in the fashionable rue Esquermoise in Lille, first opened in 1761 as a sweet shop. Now the most famous pâtisserie in Lille, they have continued to craft their own marshmallows for more than a century, and have a special counter display of elegant glass jars filled with marshmallows which customers can sample in their little *Salon de Thé*, an elegant tea room in the shop. Fortnum and Mason in Piccadilly, London, first started to produce marshmallows in 1927 which sold alongside Nougat Montelimier and Assyrian Honey Nougat.

INCREASING DEMAND

Meanwhile, marshmallows were gaining popularity in the United States and by the 1920s, they had inspired a derivative product to satisfy the sweet tooth called Fluff. A confectionery shop owner named

Left: The counter display in Meert, Lille's most famous pâtisserie.

Above: The gelatinous sap of the marshmallow plant was used by the Ancient Egyptians to make sweet desserts.

Above: Toasting marshmallows over an open fire is a treasured childhood memory for many.

Archibold Query, known for his appreciation of the marshmallow, was the first to whip up this sweet spreadable cream, consisting of corn syrup, sugar syrup, vanilla flavouring and egg whites, which contained little or none of the gelatin used in marshmallow making. Later in the 1940s Fluff hit the supermarket shelves where it was sold in cans to become a popular standby for making a variety of spreads, cake fillings and sweets. A mixture of peanut butter and Fluff squished together between pieces of bread became the official state sandwich of Massachusetts and is known affectionally as the Fluffernutter.

Nowadays, marshmallows have become a much-loved sweet for the whole family: no camping trip would

be complete without at least one feast of marshmallows toasted on twigs over an open fire. And there is nothing more warming or comforting on a cold winter's day than a mug of hot cocoa, piled high with sticky marshmallows.

NOUGAT
Another delightful confection that uses sugar and egg whites is nougat. There are two main types; white and brown. White nougat is made primarily from whipping egg whites, sugar, nuts and honey together, whereas brown nougat generally uses caramelized sugar to replace the egg whites, making it a lot thicker than white nougat. It is made slightly differently from country to country but is a popular treat, particularly at Christmas.

ARTISAN CONFECTIONS
As more and more cooks are looking to extend their cooking experience, making home-made sweets and candies has grown in popularity. There is something truly magical about homemade marshmallows and

Left: In Italy, nougat is called torrone. It comes in hard and soft varieties and has many different flavours.

nougats as the variety of flavours and colours is almost limitless and can match the weather and mood, or festivity – cranberry for Christmas, Champagne rhubarb for spring and perhaps the sharper purplish-red purées of raspberries and blueberries for summer.

Artisan marshmallows and nougats are now being made with natural ingredients such as vanilla bean paste, real chocolate and fresh fruit. The final result will provide a delicious alternative from chocolates to serve with an after-dinner espresso and as little celebratory gifts. The soft texture and airy structure of marshmallows make them perfect for party favours, and the dense, sticky texture of nougats crammed full with nuts and dried fruits will delight any recipient.

HOW TO USE THIS BOOK
The first practical section outlines everything you need to know to get started and provides detailed step-by-step guidance on how to cook both perfect marshmallow and nougat treats. The ideas that follow take these basic recipes to new heights with an irresistible mix of flavourings, fillings and textures to experiment with.

You will need a relatively small amount of baking equipment to make the recipes in this book, and you will probably have most of it already in your own kitchen. Although some items involve an initial cost, they really do make home-made sweet making easier and are a worthwhile investment for in your kitchen.

Essential Equipment

Saucepans A heavy based small- to medium-sized pan with a long handle is necessary to heat the sugar syrup.

Tins and pans Different sized tins can be used to make marshmallows although the majority of recipes here use a standard 20 x 30cm/8 x 12in, at least 4cm/1½in deep tin.

It is worth investing in good quality tins that will not rust or distort over time. If you do not have the tin called for in a recipe you can use a similar-sized tin, but be aware that you may need to make the marshmallows in more than one batch.

Mixer A good, strong mixer with a whisk attachment on a stand is a great help in making marshmallows and nougat.

Always start with a spotlessly clean, dry mixing bowl, as any residue in the bowl will affect the volume of the mixture. If a stand mixer is unavailable, the next best thing is an electric hand mixer or whisk, but it should have a strong motor, as some hand mixers are too weak to beat a large batch of marshmallow.

Sieve or strainer Essential for sifting the icing (confectioners') sugar and cornflour (cornstarch) mixture evenly.

Spatula A wide spatula is useful for incorporating flavourings into the marshmallow and a wider, flexible plastic one for scraping the mixture from the bowl into the tin.

Weighing scales With any sweet-making activity, it is important that ingredients are weighed and measured carefully. For the most accurate quantities it is worthwhile investing in a set of electronic weighing scales as they measure weights to the nearest gram or ounce.

Sugar thermometer This is an essential piece of equipment when working with hot liquids where the temperature reached is critical for the recipe. Thermometers should be clearly marked with the temperature in Celsius and/or Fahrenheit, plus the main stages for sweet-making, for example, 'hard-ball'. Sugar thermometers are very fragile and should be wrapped before storing.

Piping (pastry) bag and nozzles For effective and neat marshmallow whirls, the best results are achieved when using a large piping bag with a twelve star nozzle attachment. Piping bags are available in many forms – waterproof fabric bags that can be

Below: Shallow baking tins or pans.

Below: Electric mixer.

Below: Fine sieves or strainers.

Checking and Using a Sugar Thermometer

- Before making your syrup, you should check the accuracy of your thermometer by putting it in a pan of

water and bringing the water to a boil. Water boils at 100°C/212°F. If the temperature on your thermometer varies from this, be sure to make the same adjustment when preparing your sugar syrup.
- Sugar thermometers are very delicate pieces of equipment, and should be stored and used carefully.
- A sugar thermometer can crack if it is immersed into boiling temperatures straight from cold. To avoid this, always let it sit in a cup of hot water before immersing it in a boiling sugar syrup, just to warm the thermometer up a little.

- After use immediately place the thermometer in a bowl of hot water to dissolve and remove any sticky sugar crystals.

reused repeatedly, or disposable plastic bags that are used just once. If you are making marshmallow in several different colours it is easiest to use disposable bags, as with a fabric bag you will need to wash and dry it thoroughly between each use.

Pastry and cookie cutters These come in all sorts of shapes and sizes, and are needed for cutting out marshmallow shapes. The best ones to use are those that are deep-sided with handles on top for stamping out circular and floral confections.

Below: Wooden spoons and spatula.

Cutting tools A sharp, heavy knife with a long, narrow blade will make slicing marshmallow and nougat easier. Sturdy, sharp kitchen scissors are useful for cutting strips of marshmallow, as well as snipping baking parchment to size. A fine zester is ideal for grating citrus rind.

Measuring equipment Glass and plastic measuring jugs or cups for liquid are essential, while measuring spoons are vital for adding small quantities of ingredients. A clear plastic ruler helps to mark the size of

Below: Pastry or cookie cutters.

marshmallows and nougats accurately before cutting them for a beautiful, professional-looking result.

Bain-marie This is needed to melt ingredients such as chocolate. If you do not have a bain marie, a heatproof bowl set over a pan of simmering water will do the job.

Storage containers Most nougats and marshmallows should be stored in an airtight container, but always check the instructions on each recipe for how to store the confections.

Below: Measuring equipment.

One of the best things about making marshmallow and nougat at home is that you, as the cook, have complete control over what goes into them. The majority of the ingredients called for in this book can be purchased from a local store. A few select ingredients may be harder to find, but are worth seeking out.

Essential Ingredients

SUGARS

The most important ingredient in sweet-making is, of course, sugar. There are many different kinds of sugar. They are all derived from sugar beets or sugar cane, but are processed in different ways, so it is important to use the correct one for the recipe.

Icing (confectioners') sugar is refined sugar that has been pulverized to a delicate, white powder. Mixed in equal measures with cornflour (cornstarch) it is used to coat the tin or pan so that the marshmallow slips out easily. A fine dusting is then also applied to the finished marshmallow. Look out for the new flavoured icing sugars, which are ideal for dusting.

Caster (superfine) sugar is used when sugar needs to dissolve quite quickly. It is not as fine as icing sugar, but not as coarse as granulated white

Below: Golden syrup.

sugar. It can be used in sugar syrups, which form the basis of many confectionery recipes. White caster sugar has a clean sweet flavour, which is better used with lemon and more acidic fruit-flavoured confectionery. Golden caster sugar imparts a gentle, caramelized flavour which enhances caramel, chocolate and vanilla marshmallows, given them a slightly more neutral beige colour.

Granulated white sugar has a slightly coarser texture than caster (superfine) sugar and is also cheaper. It dissolves easily, but not so quickly that it could burn. It is the ideal sugar for melting into syrups and caramels.

Liquid glucose and corn syrup is also known as glucose syrup and helps stop the crystallization of the sugar when preparing a sugar syrup. Liquid glucose is normally made from wheat or potatoes. The US equivalent for this product is clear corn syrup, which is made from corn. It is not the same product, but can be used in the same way as liquid glucose. It is available in large supermarkets, specialist baking stores, and online.

Golden syrup and light corn syrup is a reduced by-product of sugar-cane refinement, like black treacle (molasses), but it is lighter in colour and flavour. It is an invert sugar,

created by combining a small amount of acid, such as cream of tartar or lemon juice, with a sugar syrup and heating it. This inverts, or breaks down, the sucrose into glucose and fructose, thereby reducing the size of the sugar crystals, and this fine crystal structure produces a silky smooth golden syrup. Its American equivalent is light corn syrup, which is an entirely different product but can be used in the same way, as it has the same properties.

Honey can range widely in flavour from light and sweet to dark and earthy. Lighter flavours work better with confectionery. A mild type such as lavender honey would be perfect in French nougat, for instance. It is also important not to overcook honey, as the character and flavour are altered with heat. For this reason, honey should be added at the last possible moment in the cooking process.

Below: Honey.

Making a Sugar Syrup

To make a simple sugar syrup you will need a clean, dry, heavy stainless-steel pan that is large enough to accommodate 3 to 4 times the volume of ingredients. You will also need a wooden spoon, a clean pastry brush and a sugar thermometer. You need to work quickly so gather all the ingredients and equipment you need before you start.

1 Place the amount of sugar specified in the recipe in the pan. If the recipe calls for any additional ingredient to the sugar and water, such as syrup, add that to the pan at this stage.

2 Add the quantity of water specified in the recipe to the pan. Using a large wooden spoon, slowly stir the sugar and water together over a moderate heat so as to avoid burning the mixture. Stirring is fine while the sugar is dissolving, but never stir the syrup once it is dissolved – this can cause the formation of sugar crystals.

3 Once the sugar is thoroughly dissolved, insert a sugar thermometer, increase the temperature and bring the syrup to a boil. Do not let the thermometer touch the bottom or sides of the pan, as this will affect the temperature reading. Most sugar thermometers come with a clip that can be attached to the side of the pan. If you do not have a sugar thermometer, you can test the stage of your syrup in a bowl of cold water instead (see Testing for a Set below), but using both techniques together – a thermometer and the cold-water test – will give you the most accurate and reliable results.

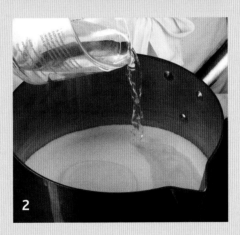

4 If any small crystals have formed along the edge of the pan at this stage, gently coax them back into the sugar syrup with a dampened pastry brush.

5 Let the mixture continue to cook until it reaches the desired stage and temperature as described in the recipe.

6 At that point, stop the cooking by removing the pan from the stove.

TIP
Speaking from a cook's painful experience, do not dip your finger into the syrup at any stage during cooking. You will get a nasty burn.

Testing for a Set

To test for the set indicated in the recipe, drop a teaspoonful of sugar syrup into a cup of very cold water and test the thickness. While the syrup is submerged in the water, it should easily form into a ball. Remove the ball from the water and hold it between your fingers. If it is sticky, but holds its shape and is rather rigid, it is at the hard-ball stage required for marshmallow.

Right: Testing for the hard-ball stage.

Above: Always use really fresh eggs.

EGGS

Use free range eggs if possible – these will inevitably taste better. A really fresh egg will separate easily and whip successfully. Large (US extra large) eggs are used in the recipes unless otherwise stated.

GELATINE

Available in a powdered form or transparent sheets or leaves, gelatine is the prime ingredient for making marshmallows. It is an animal product, but there are vegetarian alternatives available which are derived from seaweed. Powdered gelatine is used in the recipes in this book but both leaf and powder give good results. As a general rule about nine leaves of gelatine would be equivalent to 60ml/4 tbsp powdered gelatine.

To soften leaf gelatine, place the gelatine in a bowl containing 40ml/2½ tbsp cold water. Cut the sheets to fit the bowl if necessary. Leave them to soak for 4 minutes or a little longer so that they soften and swell. Squeeze out the water and add the softened leaves to the hot syrup

Beating Egg Whites

Egg whites are the essential ingredients for making confectionery like nougat and marshmallows and are best kept at room temperature before using for this purpose. Their whisked texture adds extraordinary volume and lightness and is best achieved by using an electric mixer with a whisk attachment.

Make sure the bowl and whisk are completely clean, because even a speck of egg yolk, grease or water will prevent the whites from gaining their maximum volume.

(in the marshmallow recipes) and stir to combine. Keep the soaking liquid as this is also added to the hot sugar syrup in the recipes.

To soften powdered gelatine, place 60ml/4 tbsp cold water (or the liquid indicated in the recipe) to a small shallow bowl. Sprinkle the powdered gelatine evenly over the surface and leave to soak for 4 minutes or more, by which time the gelatine will have absorbed the liquid and become

Below: To soften leaf gelatine.

swollen and spongy. Now, dissolve the gelatine by standing the bowl in a larger bowl or over a small pan partly filled with freshly boiled hot water. Leave for 3 or more minutes, until the granules become liquid and look translucent. The dissolved gelatine is now ready to use in the recipes.

TIP Timing is very important when dealing with gelatine, so have all the ingredients to hand, measured in a series of bowls, before you start.

Below: To soften powdered gelatine.

Splitting a Vanilla Pod

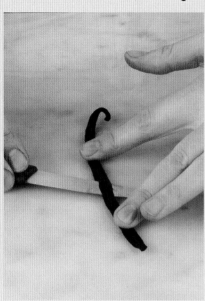

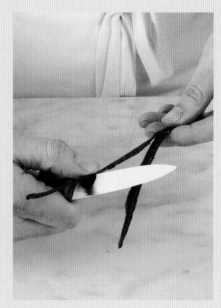

1 Lay the vanilla pod (bean) flat on a chopping board. Slice the pod lengthways using a small sharp knife, keeping the pod flat to the surface.

2 Carefully run the back of the knife along the inside of the pod to scrape out the sticky black seeds. Use the seeds immediately.

FLAVOURINGS

There are so many ways to make marshmallows look and taste wonderful, from extracts of spices and flowers to food colourings and even tea. It is always worth tasting store-bought extracts before use, as they vary greatly in concentration.

Vanilla pods (beans) come from an orchid native to Mexico. Each flower produces a single pod containing thousands of tiny seeds that lend both taste and texture to recipes. You could also use vanilla bean paste (vanilla seeds sold in a liquified paste), which mixes more evenly into beaten egg whites. You could also use a good-quality vanilla extract.

Rose water and orange blossom water are created through a distillation process. They should both be used sparingly, as they can overwhelm a delicate confection.

Flower syrups, such as rose and violet syrup, are more concentrated than flower water and are sweetened with sugar syrup. Well-flavoured flower syrups from France, Italy and the Middle East can be found in speciality stores and delicatessens.

Below: Cocoa, coffee and rose water.

Coffee beans should be preferably bought freshly roasted and whole. It is better to grind your own beans as and when they are needed wherever possible.

Chocolate and its powdered version, cocoa, come in so many different varieties that the choice may seem bewildering at first. However, there is one simple rule to remember: always choose the best quality you can find when buying chocolate for your recipes. It will make a huge difference to the end result. When making sweets, it is a matter of personal taste what percentage of cocoa is in your chosen chocolate.

Food colouring comes in paste, gel, liquid and powder form. Colourings can be found in dizzying variations at cake-decorating stores. Be careful when adding colour to a mixture; you can always add more colour, but you cannot take it away once it has been added. Liquid colours are lower in concentration than pastes or gels, and you will have to use a lot more to get the desired shade; however, using too much liquid colour can taint the flavour of your marshmallows.

Below: Food colouring paste or gel.

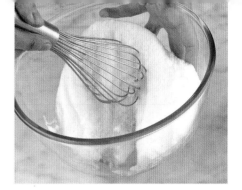

Marshmallows are made by heating sugar to the hard-ball stage (ie a temperature of 121–130°C/250–266°F). The melted sugar is combined with gelatine, colouring and flavouring, then quickly whisked into beaten egg whites. Master this standard recipe before going on to enjoy the other recipes in this book.

Making Marshmallows: a basic recipe

When making marshmallows, be sure to pour the hot sugar mixture into the egg whites in a slow, steady stream while whisking continuously, and don't over-mix, as this will compromise the lightness of the finished marshmallow. Pour the marshmallow mixture into a container greased with flavourless oil and dusting with a mixture of icing (confectioners') sugar and cornflour (cornstarch), so that once the marshmallow has set it can be removed easily. Cut the set marshmallows into pieces using an oiled knife, then dust each piece all over with a mixture of icing sugar and cornflour to prevent them from sticking to each other.

● Makes 96 2.5cm/1in pieces

vegetable oil, for greasing
50g/2oz/½ cup icing (confectioners') sugar, for dusting
50g/2oz/½ cup cornflour (cornstarch), for dusting
2 egg whites
400g/14oz/2 cups caster (superfine) sugar
15ml/1 tbsp liquid glucose or clear corn syrup
350ml/12fl oz/1½ cups cold water
60ml/4 tbsp powdered gelatine (vegetarians can substitute the gelatine with agar-agar)
30ml/2 tbsp vanilla extract

2 Whisk the egg whites until they form firm peaks (preferably in a stand mixer or with a powerful hand-held electric whisk). Set them aside. They will separate slightly, but you can whisk them up again just before you need them.

1 Lightly grease a 20cm x 30cm/ 8 x12in baking tin or pan at least 4cm/1½in deep. Combine the icing sugar and cornflour and dust the tin evenly with some of the mixture.

3 Combine the caster sugar, liquid glucose, and half of the water in a small pan over a low heat. Stir to dissolve the sugar. Bring the syrup to the boil and boil until it reaches the hard-ball stage (130°C/266°F).

4 Meanwhile, combine the gelatine with the other half of the cold water in a pan, off the heat. Just before the sugar syrup reaches the hard-ball stage, place the gelatine mixture over a low heat and stir to dissolve.

5 When the syrup reaches the correct temperature and the gelatine has dissolved, combine the two into one pan and stir (the mixture will froth up a little in the pan).

6 Turn the electric whisk on again and whisk the egg whites constantly, while pouring in the syrup and gelatine mixture in a steady stream down the inside of the bowl, for about 4–5 minutes. Stir to combine.

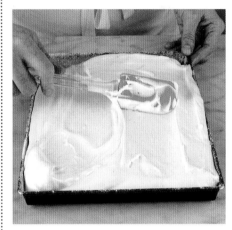

7 Turn the beater to full speed, add the vanilla extract and continue to whisk for 8–10 minutes until the meringue is stiff enough to hold its shape but still fluid enough to pour into the tin. The bottom of the bowl should be slightly warm to the touch.

8 If you wish to add a colour to your marshmallow mixture then do so at this point. You can choose to mix the colour together completely or leave it lightly streaked before pouring the mixture into the prepared pan.

9 Using a wide spatula pour the mixture into the prepared tin and smooth the top level. Allow to set at room temperature for 3 hours before cutting into pieces.

Adding Flavourings to Marshmallows

Lots of different flavours can be added to marshmallow. Vanilla, chocolate, coffee, fruit purées or flower extracts work well, and food colouring can give a fun aspect to marshmallow creations.

A raspberry purée will lend a pretty bluey-pink colour, and peppermint marshmallows look great when tinted pale green. When to add flavour to the mixture varies from recipe to recipe but it is usually added to towards the end .

Right: Dried herbs, such as lavender, or sweet violet flowers add colour as well as flavour to the marshmallow mix.

Once you have made your marshmallow mixture you can cut it into different shapes before dusting again with a mixture of icing sugar and cornflour and allowing to dry completely. The marshmallow pieces can then be stored in an airtight container if you can resist eating it all in one go!

Making Marshmallow Tips

PIPING MARSHMALLOW

If you wish, pipe the marshmallow mixture into long strips using a large pastry bag fitted with a 12 star nozzle.

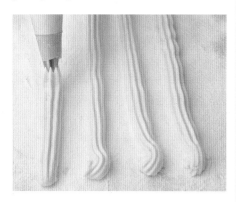

1 Fill the pastry bag with the marshmallow mixture and, working quickly, pipe long tubes onto a large flat baking tray oiled and dusted with the icing sugar and cornflour mix.

2 When the mixture sets (about 3 hours) cut into short 2.5cm/1in pieces with an oiled knife or scissors. To serve, dust lightly with icing sugar and cornflour.

CUTTING MARSHMALLOWS

Marshmallow is solid enough to be cut into neat squares to achieve a professional finish. It is very sticky, so can pose a challenge to cut it well. Dust the work surface with icing (confectioners') sugar and cornflour (cornstarch) before you start, and have some more of this mixture on hand with which to dust the pieces after you have cut it.

1 Use a small, sharp paring knife to neaten the edges of the marshmallow while still in the tin or pan, then invert the tin on to the surface dusted with the icing sugar and cornflour mixture. Carefully unmould the marshmallow mixture onto the prepared work surface.

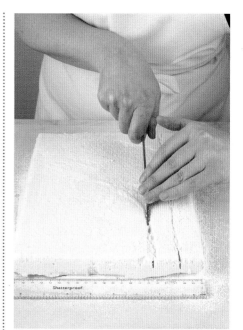

2 For a clean cut, lightly oil the blade of a long, sharp heavy flat-edged bladed kitchen knife or Chinese cleaver. Clean and oil the blade after each cut to prevent the marshmallow from sticking (wipe off the excess oil from the blades with the kitchen paper). First cut the marshmallow into long strips then, using sharp kitchen scissors, cut the strips into uniform squares.

3 Dust a little of the extra icing sugar and cornflour mixture over the pieces. Leave to dry out for a few hours and then store in an airtight container.

MARSHMALLOW SHAPES

Apart from cutting into squares, once marshmallow has set, you can use cookie cutters to cut it into different shapes. A range of pretty, deep-sided cookie cutters are available from kitchen stores. Lightly oil the cutter to achieve a consistently sharp effect.

Left: Make marshmallow twists by cutting fine strips of marshmallow of different colours and twisting them together into long strands. Then cut into small bitesize pieces.

Above: Marshmallows may also be cut and shaped with lightly oiled deep-sided cookie cutters.

Left: It is possible to pipe the soft marshmallow mixture into attractive whirls. For best results, use a large pastry bag fitted with a 12 star nozzle.

STORING MARSHMALLOWS

Once the marshmallows have dried out thoroughly, store them in an airtight container, layered with baking parchment cut to the same size as the box. The marshmallows should keep for about 2 weeks.

TIP

When making marshmallows, bear in mind that the marshmallow mixture will taste sweeter hot than cold, so don't worry if the warm marshmallow mixture tastes almost too sweet – the flavour will change when the mixture cools.

Dusting Marshmallows

When dusting the tops of the marshmallow with freeze-dried raspberries, finely powdered meringue, or crushed finely powdered amaretti biscuits, it's best to cut the mallow slab into pieces, separating the squares only very slightly. Then dust the pieces with the powdered ingredients and leave them for several hours to dry out before separating the marshmallow pieces completely. This way you get a more uniform look.

Nougat contains egg whites but no gelatine, and comes in different textures, rangeing from chewy to brittle. Iranian nougat is on the more brittle, chalky side. Chewy nougat from Europe contains honey, golden (light corn) syrup or glucose syrup to stop sugar crystals from forming, giving it a lovely soft texture.

Making Nougat: a basic recipe

Nougat gets its distinctive texture from the mixture of sugar, water and glucose or corn syrup. It is slightly different in every country so no two recipes are exactly the same. Here is a basic recipe, to which you can add different nuts or fruits.

● Makes about 1kg/2¼lb

rice paper
2 egg whites
375g/13oz/scant 2 cups caster (superfine) sugar
15ml/1 tbsp liquid glucose or clear corn syrup
100ml/3½fl oz/scant ½ cup water
120ml/4fl oz/½ cup honey
grapeseed or groundnut (peanut) oil, for greasing

1   First line a cake tin or pan with edible rice paper. Put the egg whites into the bowl of an electric mixer (preferably on a stand), whip them to stiff peaks and leave them to rest. Ensure the bowl is scrupulously clean before adding the egg whites.

3   Turn the electric stand mixer on, and drizzle the syrup into the whipped egg whites in a steady stream until the nougat thickens.

2   Combine the sugar, glucose syrup and water in a pan. Cook until the mixture reaches 138°C/280°F. Warm the honey in a separate pan until it is just boiling, then add it to the sugar syrup and bring the mixture up to 143°C/290°F.

4   Pour the mixture into the prepared tin. Cover with rice paper, then place a board and some weights on top. Leave it to set overnight.

CUTTING NOUGAT

Nougat is traditionally cut into even bite-sized pieces before storing.

1 Remove the weights from the nougat. Turn the nougat out onto a sheet of baking parchment. Lightly oil a large sharp knife and trim away any rough edges.

2 Cut the slab into slices and then into individual pieces. It is important to use a very sharp knife, because you may be cutting through large pieces of fruit or nuts. Wrap the pieces in individual pieces of baking parchment or pack in a paper-lined box or tin. Nougat keeps well for 3 weeks.

Adding Extra Ingredients to Nougat

Toasted nuts, orange blossom water and candied fruits make delicious additions to this basic nougat. Fold them into the mixture before spooning it into the prepared tin or pan.

NOUGAT ICE CREAM

A basic nougat recipe can also be adapted to create a superb ice cream, especially when served with iced liqueurs as an elegant dessert.

● Serves 6 to 8

6–8 sheets rice paper
3 egg whites
150g/5oz/1¼ cups icing (confectioners') sugar, sifted
300ml/½ pint/1¼ cups double (heavy) cream
10ml/2 tsp orange flower water
50g/2oz/½ cup hazelnuts, roughly chopped
50g/2oz/½ cup pistachio nuts, roughly chopped
50g/2oz/½ cup candied peel, in fine slices

1 Line the base and sides of a 28 x 18 x 4cm/11 x 7 x 1½in cake tin or pan with clear film (plastic wrap), then line with four pieces of rice paper, folding the paper into the corners.

2 Put the egg whites and icing sugar into a large, heatproof bowl. Place it over a pan of simmering water and whisk for 5 minutes or until the meringue is very thick. Take off the heat and continue whisking until soft peaks form.

3 In a separate bowl, whip the cream and orange flower water lightly, then fold in the meringue.

4 Spoon half the meringue mixture into the lined cake tin, easing it into the corners. Sprinkle the meringue with half the nuts and candied peel. Cover with the remaining meringue mixture.

5 Sprinkle with the remaining nuts and fruit. Cover with two more sheets of rice paper and freeze for at least 6 hours or overnight until it is completely firm.

6 Carefully turn the ice cream out of the tin and peel off the clear film. If the base of the ice cream is soft, cover it with the remaining two sheets of rice paper, pressing it on to the ice cream so that it sticks.

7 Cut into small squares or triangles, arrange on individual plates and serve immediately.

A food gift of confectionery can be the perfect present to give to a friend or loved one, especially when it is home-made and put together creatively. Presenting your artisan treats in pretty packages adds to the fun. Here are some practical and decorative ideas for making the most of sweet gifts.

Presentation Ideas

QUICK AND EASY
- Line a container with colourful tissue paper, then add a piece of waxed paper to stop the oils seeping through.
- Keep any small gift boxes you are given and reuse them by covering them with new, colourful papers.
- Antique plates or bowls are easy to use. Wrap the entire container in a big square of cellophane gathered together on top with a ribbon.
- Vintage plates are easy to find at charity shops (thrift stores) at great prices, and they become a reusable part of the gift.
- Add a bow in a matching colour. Satin and grosgrain ribbons make a beautiful package, but you can also use raffia, string or cord.
- Clean old mason jars or small Kilner jars, and pack full of bite-sized marshmallow or nougat pieces, topped off with a pretty ribbon
- Make simple cones out of colourful paper and top full with little marshmallow squares to hand out as party bags.
- Package the confectionery at the last minute to keep it at its best.

Tying a Perfect Bow

Tied with skill, a bow can create a simple but professional finish for a home-made gift.

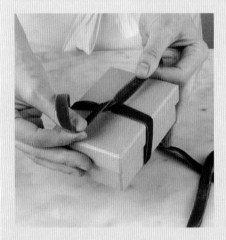

1 Hold one end of the ribbon in the centre of the top of the gift box, with enough remaining at the end for one loop of the bow.

2 Wrap the ribbon around the box and, when it meets the centre, turn it 90° and wrap it the other way, bringing the ribbon back to the top. Secure it by wrapping it over and then back under the ribbon in the centre so you have a cross on top.

3 Tie the two ends of ribbon into a neat bow, loosely at first to make sure you make the loops the same size, then pull it tight once you are happy with the shape. Trim the ends of the ribbons, if necessary, to make them the same length.

Right: Fill a clear cellophane bag with marshmallows and place them in an antique coffee cup. Add a label marked with the name of recipient and tie it with a pretty ribbon. There are shops who specialize in selling ribbons that are worth looking out for. Antique French ribbons set a style and can be particularly beautiful.

Above: For a natural effect use simple cream and brown cardboard gift boxes, layered with rice paper and tied with pastel coloured ribbons or twine. Note the flavouring on a hand-written label.

Above: Stationery shops are full of sweet little boxes which are perfect for giving, packed with little shaped marshmallows.

Above: Fill little cellophane bags with pretty pink and white marshmallows made with vanilla and fresh raspberry flavourings. Tie the tops with plain or patterned coloured ribbons or coloured plastic clothes pegs and present each one in a stripy ice-cream carton.

Above: Impress your dinner party guests by presenting them with a selection of marshmallows nestled in paper cake cups then placed inside cellophane bags secured at the tops with fine organza ribbons.

Classic Marshmallows

These traditional marshmallows will bring back
treasured memories of childhood. They include
the best-loved favourites, such as vanilla and
peppermint as well as the popular fruit flavours
of raspberry, blueberry and maple syrup.
Their simplicity is what makes them memorable
and these will be tastiest when made
with top-quality ingredients.

Wonderfully fluffy and delicious, home-made marshmallows are nothing like the store-bought version. The texture is completely different because these are meant to be eaten within days, rather than months, and are not full of preservatives. You can add many flavours and colours to ring the changes.

Vanilla Marshmallows

- Makes 96 2.5cm/1in pieces

vegetable oil, for greasing
50g/2oz/½ cup icing
   (confectioners') sugar, for dusting
50g/2oz/½ cup cornflour
   (cornstarch), for dusting
2 egg whites
400g/14oz/2 cups caster
   (superfine) sugar
15ml/1 tbsp liquid glucose or clear
   corn syrup
30ml/2 tbsp vanilla bean paste or
   vanilla extract
350ml/12fl oz/1½ cups cold water
60ml/4 tbsp powdered gelatine

COOK'S TIP
Dust them liberally with cornflour and icing sugar to stop them sticking together.

1 Prepare a 20cm x 30cm/ 8 x12in baking tin or pan at least 4cm/1½in deep following the instructions on page 14.

2 Whisk the egg whites until they form firm peaks (preferably in a stand mixer). Set aside.

3 Combine the caster sugar, liquid glucose, the vanilla bean paste or extract, and half of the water in a small pan over a low heat. Stir to dissolve the sugar.

4 Bring the syrup to the boil and boil until it reaches the hard-ball stage (130°C/266°F).

5 Meanwhile, combine the gelatine with the other half of the cold water in a small pan, off the heat. Just before the sugar syrup reaches the hard-ball stage, place the gelatine mixture over a low heat and stir to dissolve the gelatine.

6 When the syrup reaches the correct temperature and the gelatine has dissolved, combine the two into one pan and stir off the heat.

7 Turn the electric whisk on again, whisk the egg whites constantly, and add the syrup and gelatine mixture following the method on page 15.

8 Turn the beater to full speed, add the vanilla extract and continue to whisk for a further 8–10 minutes until the meringue is stiff enough to hold its own shape while remaining thin enough to flow easily into the tin.

9 Using a wide spatula pour the mixture into the prepared tin and smooth the top level. Allow to set at room temperature for 3 hours.

10 Prepare the work surface, turn the marshmallow out and cut into squares as on page 16. Allow to dry out for 2 hours and dust again.

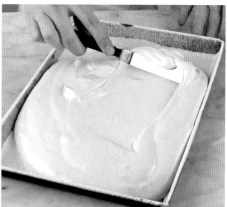

The delightful minty green of these fresh-tasting sweets comes from food colouring. Here, traditional liquid food colouring is used, but if you are using gel or paste, you will only need the tiniest amount. The green colour should be subtle and light, so take care not to use too much!

Peppermint Marshmallows

● Makes 96 2.5cm/1in pieces

vegetable oil, for greasing
50g/2oz/½ cup icing (confectioners') sugar, for dusting
50g/2oz/½ cup cornflour (cornstarch), for dusting
2 egg whites
400g/14oz/2 cups caster (superfine) sugar
15ml/1 tbsp liquid glucose or clear corn syrup
350ml/12fl oz/1½ cups cold water
60ml/4 tbsp powdered gelatine
10ml/2 tsp peppermint extract
2.5ml/½ tsp liquid green food colouring, a drop of gel colouring, or a tiny dab of colouring paste from the end of a cocktail stick (toothpick)

1 Prepare a 20cm x 30cm/ 8 x12in baking tin or pan at least 4cm/1½in deep following the instructions on page 14.

2 Whisk the egg whites until they form firm peaks (preferably using a stand mixer). Set aside.

3 Combine the caster sugar, liquid glucose and half of the water in a small, heavy pan over a low heat. Stir to dissolve the sugar.

4 Bring the syrup to the boil and boil until it reaches the hard-ball stage (130°C/266°F).

5 Meanwhile, combine the gelatine with the rest of the cold water in a small pan, off the heat. Just before the sugar syrup reaches the hard-ball stage, place the gelatine mixture over a low heat and stir to dissolve the gelatine.

6 When the syrup reaches the correct temperature and the gelatine has dissolved, pour the gelatine mixture into the syrup and stir to combine. Add the peppermint extract and green food colouring, and stir.

7 Turn the electric whisk on again, whisk the egg whites constantly, and add the syrup and gelatine mixture following the method on page 15.

8 Turn the beater to full speed and continue to whisk for a further 8–10 minutes until the meringue is stiff enough to hold its own shape but flows easily into the tin.

9 Using a spatula pour the mixture into the prepared tin and smooth level. Allow to set for 3 hours.

10 Prepare the work surface, turn the marshmallow out and cut into squares as on page 16. Allow to dry out for 2 hours and dust again.

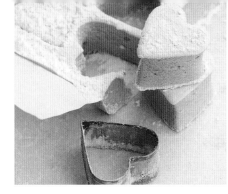

You can add almost any flavour to marshmallows. Berries are especially wonderful, because the acidity in the fruit balances the sweetness of the fluffy, sugary mass. The colour of the berries also transfers to the finished confections, in this case creating a delicate, soft pink.

Raspberry Heart Marshmallows

● Makes 45 hearts

vegetable oil, for greasing
50g/2oz/½ cup icing (confectioners') sugar, for dusting
50g/2oz/½ cup cornflour (cornstarch), for dusting
2 egg whites
400g/14oz/2 cups caster (superfine) sugar
15ml/1 tbsp liquid glucose or clear corn syrup
75ml/6fl oz/¾ cup cold water
60ml/4 tbsp powdered gelatine
200ml/7fl oz/scant 1 cup puréed raspberries, strained
10ml/2 tsp vanilla extract

COOK'S TIPS
Cut these into heart shapes with lightly oiled cookie cutters.

1   Prepare a 20cm x 30cm/ 8 x12in baking tin or pan at least 4cm/1½in deep following the instructions on page 14.

2   Whisk the egg whites until they form firm peaks (preferable using a stand mixer). Set aside.

3   Combine the sugar, liquid glucose and 75ml/5 tbsp of the cold water in a small pan over a low heat. Stir to dissolve the sugar.

4   Bring the syrup to the boil and boil until it reaches the hard-ball stage (130°C/266°F).

5   Meanwhile, combine the gelatine with the rest of the cold water in a small pan, off the heat. Just before the sugar syrup reaches the hard-ball stage, place the gelatine mixture over a low heat and stir until the gelatine has dissolved.

6   When the syrup has reached the correct temperature, pour the gelatine mixture into the syrup and stir. Add the raspberry purée and the vanilla extract and stir to combine.

7   Turn the whisk on again, whisk the egg whites constantly, and add the syrup, raspberry and gelatine mixture following the method on page 15.

8   Turn the beater to full speed and whisk for a further 8–10 minutes until the meringue is stiff enough to hold its own shape while remaining thin enough to flow easily into the tin.

9   Using a wide spatula pour the mixture into the prepared tin and smooth the top level. Allow to set at room temperature for 3 hours.

10 Prepare the work surface, turn the marshmallow out and cut into shapes as on page 17. Allow to dry out for 2 hours and dust again.

This classic recipe for pretty two-tone marshmallows is a joy to make. The end result is wonderful in both texture and colour. The combination of pink and yellow is delightful, but you could always choose other colours, if you prefer. Try twisting them or tying them into pretzel-like knots.

Marshmallow Sticks

- Makes about 900g/2lb

vegetable oil, for greasing
50g/2oz/½ cup icing
   (confectioners') sugar, for dusting
50g/2oz/½ cup cornflour
   (cornstarch), for dusting
2 egg whites
400g/14oz/2 cups caster
   (superfine) sugar
15ml/1 tbsp liquid glucose or clear
   corn syrup
375ml/13fl oz/generous 1½ cups
   cold water
60ml/4 tbsp powdered gelatine
5ml/1 tsp vanilla extract
3 drops pink food colouring
3 drops yellow food colouring

1 Prepare a 20cm x 30cm/ 8 x12in baking tin or pan at least 4cm/1½in deep following the instructions on page 14.

2 Whisk the egg whites until they form firm peaks. Set aside.

3 Combine the sugar, liquid glucose, and half of the water in a small pan over low heat. Stir to dissolve the sugar.

4 Bring the syrup to the boil and boil until it reaches the hard-ball stage (130°C/266°F).

5 Meanwhile, using the remaining water, prepare the gelatine following the method on page 15.

6 When the syrup reaches the correct temperature and the gelatine has dissolved, pour the gelatine mixture into the syrup and stir to combine. Add the vanilla extract.

7 Turn the electric whisk on again, whisk the egg whites constantly, and add the syrup and gelatine mixture following the method on page 15.

8 Divide the mixture between two bowls and add a different food colouring to each. Continue to whisk for a further 8–10 minutes until the meringue is stiff enough to hold its own shape while remaining thin enough to flow easily into the tin. (You will need to do this one at a time, working quickly, if you only have one mixer or whisk.)

9 Pour the yellow mixture into the baking tray and spread it out evenly. Pour the pink mixture on top. Allow to set for 3 hours.

10 Prepare the work surface, turn the marshmallow out and cut into sticks as on page 16. Allow to dry out for 2 hours and dust again to stop them from sticking together.

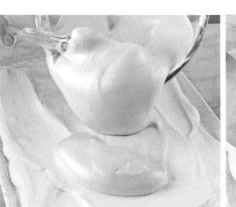

These light and fragrant mouthfuls of pale pink mousse are flavoured with rose water and will simply melt in the mouth. As with all marshmallows, either serve them immediately, or store them in an airtight container. For a pretty gift, wrap some in cellophane, add a few tiny rose buds and finish with a ribbon.

Rose Water Marshmallows

- Makes 96 2.5cm/1in pieces

vegetable oil, for greasing
50g/2oz/½ cup icing
  (confectioners') sugar, for dusting
50g/2oz/½ cup cornflour
  (cornstarch), for dusting
2 egg whites
400g/14oz/2 cups caster (superfine)
  sugar
15ml/1 tbsp liquid glucose or clear
  corn syrup
375ml/13fl oz/generous 1½ cups
  cold water
60ml/4 tbsp powdered gelatine
45ml/3 tbsp rose water
3 drops pink food colouring

COOK'S TIP
If you prefer, substitute the rose water with orange blossom water.

1 Prepare a 20cm x 30cm/ 8 x12in baking tin or pan at least 4cm/1½in deep following the instructions on page 14.

2 Whisk the egg whites until they form firm peaks (preferably using a stand mixer). Set aside.

3 Combine the caster sugar, liquid glucose and half of the water in a small, heavy pan over a low heat. Stir to dissolve the sugar.

4 Bring the syrup to the boil and boil until it reaches the hard-ball stage (130°C/266°F).

5 Meanwhile, combine the gelatine with the rest of the cold water in a small pan, off the heat. Just before the sugar syrup reaches the hard-ball stage, place the gelatine mixture over a low heat and stir to dissolve the gelatine.

6 When the syrup reaches the correct temperature and the gelatine has dissolved, pour the gelatine mixture into the syrup and stir.

7 Add the rose water and pink food colouring, and stir.

8 Turn the electric whisk on again and whisk the egg whites while pouring the hot syrup in a thin, steady stream down the inside of the bowl, for about 4–5 minutes. Continue to whisk for a further 8–10 minutes until the meringue is stiff enough to hold its own shape while remaining thin enough to flow easily into the tin.

9 Pour the marshmallow into the prepared baking tray and smooth the top. Leave to set for 3 hours.

10 Prepare the work surface, turn the marshmallow out and cut into squares as on page 16. Allow to dry out for 2 hours and dust again.

Fresh blueberries are added to these moreish marshmallows. Blueberries have a frosty bloom that intensifies their blueness and their purplish reddish juices tint these marshmallows prettily. Pure maple syrup, so popular in bakes and candies in New England, provides the finishing flavour.

Blueberry Marshmallows

• Makes 96 2.5cm/1in pieces

vegetable oil, for greasing
50g/2oz/½ cup icing
   (confectioners') sugar, for dusting
50g/2oz/½ cup cornflour
   (cornstarch), for dusting
175g/6oz fresh blueberries
juice of 1 lemon
90ml/6 tbsp maple syrup
2 large egg whites
400g/14oz caster (superfine) sugar
15ml/1 tbsp liquid glucose or clear
   corn syrup
350ml/12fl oz/1½ cups cold water
60ml/4 tbsp powdered gelatine

COOK'S TIP
If you prefer, mix the blueberry purée evenly into the mix for a soft purple tint.

1 Prepare a 20cm x 30cm/ 8 x12in baking tin or pan at least 4cm/1½in deep following the instructions on page 14.

2 Tip the blueberries, lemon juice and maple syrup into a pan and leave them to simmer for 7–8 minutes. Remove the fruit, draining the liquid back into the pan then reduce the juices until slightly thickened for a further 2–3 minutes. Leave to cool.

3 Mash the fruit gently with a fork, then purée the blueberry and maple syrup juices through a sieve or strainer.

4 Whisk the egg whites until they form firm peaks (preferably using a stand mixer). Set aside.

5 Add the sugar, liquid glucose and half of the water to a pan and cook until the syrup reaches the hard-ball stage (130°C/266°F) following the method on page 14.

6 Meanwhile, using the remaining water prepare the gelatine following the method on page 15.

7 When the sugar syrup is ready, remove it from the heat. Stir in the dissolved gelatine.

8 Continue to beat the egg white while pouring the hot syrup in a thin stream down the inside of the bowl, then continue to beat the mixture for a further 8–10 minutes until it is stiff enough to hold its own shape and liquid enough to flow into the tin.

9 Quickly mix in the cooled puréed blueberries until the marshmallow has fine streaks. Pour into the prepared tin and leave to set for 3 hours to set.

10 Prepare the work surface, turn the marshmallow out and cut into squares as on page 16. Allow to dry out for 2 hours and dust again. Pack into airtight boxes layered with wax paper.

Kid's Marshmallows

The fun ideas and creative decorations in this
chapter are sure to delight youngsters of all ages.
From Rocky Road Pops and Lemon Sherbert
UFO's to Fluffernutter Lollipops and Angel
Marshmallow Cornets these delectable
creations are perfect for birthday parties,
special tea-time treats and any other time
you want to raise a smile on a little one's face.

Lemon fruit curd and lemon juice give a fresh zesty flavour to these large marshmallows, which are decorated with pastel-coloured sherbet-filled flying saucers. You will need a circular deep-sided cookie cutter to create the marshmallow rounds. Lightly oiling the cutter will ensure a smooth finish.

Lemon Sherbet U.F.O.'s

● Makes 35 large marshmallows

vegetable oil, for greasing
50g/2oz/½ cup icing (confectioners') sugar, for dusting
50g/2oz/½ cup cornflour (cornstarch), for dusting
2 large egg whites
400g/14oz/2 cups caster (superfine) sugar
15ml/1tbsp liquid glucose or clear corn syrup
350ml/12fl oz/1½ cups cold water
60ml/4 tbsp powdered gelatine
juice of 1 lemon
90ml/6 tbsp home-made lemon curd, or a quality store-bought one
115g/4oz yellow sherbet powder, plus 15ml/1 tbsp extra lemon sherbet powder, to decorate
35 pastel-coloured sherbet flying saucers (satellite wafers)
coloured lollipop sticks, to serve

1 Prepare a 20cm x 30cm/ 8 x12in baking tin or pan at least 4cm/1½in deep following the instructions on page 14.

2 Whisk the egg whites until they form firm peaks. Set aside.

3 Add the sugar, liquid glucose and half of the water to a small pan set over a low heat and stir to dissolve the sugar. Bring the mixture to a steady boil and continue to heat until the syrup reaches the hard-ball stage (130°C/266°F).

4 Meanwhile, using the remaining water prepare the gelatine following the method on page 15.

5 When the sugar syrup is ready, take it off the heat and pour the dissolved gelatine into the hot syrup (the mixture will bubble up a little in the pan). Stir in the lemon juice to combine.

6 Turn the beater to full speed while pouring the hot syrup in a steady stream down the inside of the bowl, until it is all combined, then continue to beat for about a further 8–10 minutes, until the marshmallow mixture is stiff enough to hold its own shape, while thin enough to flow easily into the tin. Quickly fold in the lemon curd and sherbet powder.

7 Pour the mixture into the prepared tin and smooth it level. Sprinkle the remaining 15ml/1 tbsp sherbet over the top and leave for 3 hours to set.

8 Prepare the work surface as on page 16 then, using a palette knife, loosen the edges of the marshmallow and turn it out. Lightly oil a 4cm/1½in round cookie cutter and stamp out circles. Dust the tops with some of the icing sugar and cornflour mix. Leave to dry for a few hours. Place a flying saucer on each marshmallow and secure with a lollipop stick.

Gorgeous whipped marshmallow cornets, sprinkled with freeze-dried strawberries and studded with little diamond jellies will delight any child and are perfect to serve at a party or for a special dessert. You will require two large pastry bags fitted with two 12 star nozzles and a wide flexible plastic spatula.

Angel Marshmallow Cornets

• Makes 21 cornets

2 egg whites
15ml/1 tbsp vanilla extract
400g/14oz/2 cups caster (superfine) sugar
15ml/1 tbsp liquid glucose or clear corn syrup
350ml/12floz/1½ cups cold water
60ml/4 tbsp powdered gelatine
21 flat-bottomed ice cream cornets
75g/3oz carton of jelly diamonds
1 small carton of freeze-dried strawberry sprinkles or sprinkles of your own choice, or popping candy, optional

COOK'S TIP
When piping, work at a steady pace before the marshmallow cools and begins to set.

1 Prepare the piping bags. Stand them upright, inside tall measuring jugs or similar sized containers, and fold the tops of the bags over the rim of the containers to hold them steady.

2 Whisk the egg whites with the vanillla extract in a grease-free bowl until they form firm peaks (preferably in a stand mixer). Set aside.

3 Add the sugar, liquid glucose, and half of the water (175ml/6fl oz/¾ cup) to a small to medium heavy pan. Place the pan over a low heat and gently stir to dissolve the sugar. Bring the mixture gradually to the boil and continue to heat steadily until the syrup reaches the hard-ball stage (130°C/266°F).

4 Meanwhile, add the remaining water to a bowl and sprinkle over the powdered gelatine. Allow the gelatine to dissolve suspended over a pan of hot water.

5 When the sugar syrup is ready, take it off the heat and pour the dissolved gelatine into the syrup.

6 Turn the beater to full speed while pouring the hot syrup in a thin, steady stream down the inside of the bowl, for about 4-5 minutes. Continue beating for a further 8–10 minutes until the meringue is stiff enough to hold its own shape, while thin enough to transfer to the piping bags.

7 Using the wide flexible spatula, carefully transfer the marshmallow mixture into the large pastry bags fitted with the nozzles. Pipe equally into the ice cream cones, so the mixture fills each one and is about 4cm/1½in above the rims, swirling the tops and releasing the pressure as you pull up to form a peak.

8 Decorate with the sweets and sprinkles. Leave to set at room temperature for 2 hours.

Popcorn caramel and creamy peanut butter melted together with vanilla marshmallows make delicious sticky party treats that are quite irresistible for the kiddie's and shush... possibly most of the adults. Double the quantity of ingredients for a large party – they are guaranteed to disappear quickly.

Fluffernutter Lollipops

● Makes 12 lollipops

40 vanilla marshmallows (see basic marshmallow recipe, page 14)
115g/4oz ready-made plain popcorn
50g/2oz/3½ tbsp smooth peanut butter
12 lolly (popsicle) sticks, to serve
for the caramel sauce
65g/2½oz/5 tbsp light brown sugar
65g/2½oz/5 tbsp butter
65ml/4½ tbsp double (heavy) cream

COOK'S TIP
When serving lolly sticks to children make sure that there are no sharp points.

1   Pour the popcorn into a large mixing bowl.

2   Add the marshmallows to a medium-sized pan, and set over a low heat for 4 minutes until the marshmallows begin to melt. Reduce the heat to low and stir occasionally until the marshmallows look creamy and melted. Keep a close eye on the mixture to make sure it doesn't burn.

3   Remove from the heat and leave to cool for 10 minutes.

4   Meanwhile, make the caramel sauce. In a heavy-based pan, gently heat the sugar and butter until the butter has melted and the sugar is dissolved. Add the cream and heat until bubbling, stirring continually.

5   Lightly stir the peanut butter and 60ml/4 tbsp caramel sauce together, then stir into the melted marshmallows until the mixture looks streaky.

6   Pour the mixture over the popcorn and mix gently to combine. Leave for a further 4 minutes, stirring to distribute the ingredients evenly, until the popcorn begins to look sticky (about another 4 minutes).

7   Divide the mixture evenly into 12 mounds, then press a lolly stick into each one. Lightly press to form into tall ball shapes, then leave them to set on silicone paper for 3 or 4 hours.

8   Eat freshly made if possible, served on their own or in paper cups to catch any sticky droppings.

COOK'S TIP
If you prefer, you can can buy ready-made caramel or toffee sauce.

These pops take their inspiration from rocky road ice cream and are packed with cherries, chocolate and marshmallows. Two types of cookies are included to add extra crunch for a special treat. You only need to cut small squares of this slice for each pop as the mixture is very rich.

Rocky Road Marshmallow Pops

● Makes 28 pops

400g/14oz plain (semisweet)
  chocolate, chopped
125g/4¼oz/8½ tbsp butter
100g/3¾oz/scant 2 cups digestive
  biscuits (graham crackers), crushed
100g/3¾oz/scant 2 cups chocolate
  sandwich cookies, crushed
125g/5oz mini marshmallows
150g/5oz/scant ¾ cup glacé
  (candied) cherries, halved
100g/3¾oz/scant ½ cup glacé
  (candied) cherries, halved
100g/3¾oz white chocolate, melted
28 wooden skewers, to serve

1 Grease and line a 28 x 18cm/ 11 x 7in deep rectangular cake tin or pan.

2 To make the chocolate slice, place the chocolate and butter in a large heatproof bowl set over a pan of gently simmering water, taking care that the water does not touch the bottom of the bowl.

3 Stir until the butter and chocolate are melted and blended, then remove from the heat.

4 Add the crushed digestive biscuits, crushed chocolate cookies, half the mini marshmallows and glacé cherries to the melted chocolate mixture and combine well to coat everything in the chocolate.

5 Spoon the mixture into the tin and smooth it out flat using a spoon, making sure the mixture goes into all the corners.

6 For the topping, sprinkle the glacé cherries and the remaining mini marshmallows over the top. Drizzle over the white chocolate in thin lines using a spoon. Leave to set in the refrigerator.

7 To serve, remove the slice from the tin and cut into 28 squares. Insert a wooden skewer into each square.

COOK'S TIP
Take care when serving cake pops to children to blunt the ends of the skewers.

These fun marshmallow pops are sure to be a hit at a children's party. They can be made with almost any flavour you like. Here they are made with pineapple and coconut – tastes that transport you instantly to sunny climes and tropical beaches!

Pina Colada Marshmallow Swirls

● Makes 15 swirls

50g/2oz/½ cup icing (confectioners') sugar, for dusting
50g/2oz/½ cup cornflour (cornstarch), for dusting
500g/1¼lb/2½ cups caster (superfine) sugar
60ml/4 tbsp liquid glucose or clear corn syrup
350ml/12fl oz/1½ cups pineapple juice
25g/1oz powdered gelatine
50ml/2fl oz/¼ cup coconut milk
a few drops of yellow food colouring gel
15 lollipop sticks, to serve

1 Prepare a baking tin or pan at least 4cm/1½in deep following the instructions on page 14.

2 Combine the caster sugar, liquid glucose, and 250ml/8fl oz/1 cup of the pineapple juice in a small pan over a low heat. Stir to dissolve the sugar.

3 Bring the syrup to the boil and boil until it reaches the hard-ball stage (130°C/266°F).

4 Meanwhile, combine the gelatine with the remaining pineapple juice and coconut milk in a small pan, off the heat. Just before the sugar syrup reaches the hard-ball stage, place the gelatine mixture over a low heat and stir to dissolve the gelatine.

5 When the syrup reaches the correct temperature and the gelatine has dissolved, pour the gelatine mixture into the syrup and stir to combine.

6 Whisk on medium-high for about 8–10 minutes, until the mixture is stiff enough to hold its own shape while remaining thin enough to flow easily into the tin.

7 Pour half of the marshmallow mixture into the tin. Smooth level.

8 Stir the yellow food colouring gel into the remaining marshmallow, mixing to a uniform yellow colour. Pour the yellow marshmallow on top of the white marshmallow. Leave to set at room temperature for 3 hours.

9 Dust the top of the marshmallow with icing sugar and cornflour, invert it on to a flat surface. Dust again.

10 Cut 1cm/½in-wide long strips of the marshmallow using icing sugar-dusted scissors, dusting the exposed cut sides with a little icing sugar. Roll up the strips into spirals. Secure each with a stick.

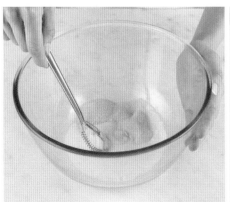

Gourmet Marshmallows

If you thought marshmallows were just
for children then this chapter will quickly change
your mind. There is plenty here to tempt grown-up
tastebuds, with flavourings like chocolate
honeycomb, salted caramel, Matcha green tea,
toasted coconut and maya gold chocolate, as
well as a selection of fruity delights, such as
Rhubarb and Angelica Marshmallows
and Seville Orange Marshmallows.

Make pretty creamy apricot coloured marshmallows with the delicate almond flavour of finely crushed amaretti biscuits. Make sure though, that the apricots are ripe, sweet and full-flavoured for the best results. Add a few drops of natural apricot food colouring if you like.

Apricot & Amaretti Marshmallows

● Makes 96 2.5cm/1in pieces

vegetable oil, for greasing
50g/2oz/½ cup icing
 (confectioners') sugar, for dusting
50g/2oz/½ cup cornflour
 (cornstarch), for dusting
4–5 large soft ripe apricots, stoned
 (about 350g/12oz fruit)
15ml/1 tbsp golden caster
 (superfine) sugar
2 large egg whites
400g/14oz/2 cups caster (superfine)
 sugar
15ml/1 tbsp liquid glucose, or clear
 corn syrup
350ml/12fl oz/1½ cups cold water
60ml/4 tbsp powdered gelatine
6–7 drops apricot, natural food
 colouring, optional
100g/4oz/4 cup amaretti biscuits,
 very finely crushed

1 Prepare a 20cm x 30cm/ 8 x 12in baking tin or pan at least 4cm/1½in deep following the instructions on page 14.

2 Add the apricots with the sugar and 30ml/2 tbsp water to a pan. Cook over a moderate heat until the mixture reduces to a thick pulp. Purée the fruit through a sieve or strainer. Reserve 115g/4oz of puréed fruit.

3 Whisk the egg whites until they form stiff peaks. Set aside.

4 Add the caster sugar, liquid glucose and half of the water to a pan over a low heat and stir to dissolve the sugar. Bring the mixture gradually to a steady boil and cook without stirring until the syrup reaches the hard-ball stage (130°C/266°F).

5 Meanwhile, using the remaining water, prepare the gelatine following the method on page 15.

6 When the sugar syrup is ready, remove it from the heat. Stir in the liquefied gelatine and stir to combine with the food colouring, if using.

7 Turn the beater full speed while pouring the hot syrup in a thin steady stream down the inside of the bowl, until it is all combined, then continue to whisk the mixture for a further 8–10 minutes until the mixture is stiff enough to hold its own shape.

8 Combine the apricot purée and half of the crushed amaretti biscuits until just mixed (do not over-mix or you will slacken the mixture).

9 Pour into the prepared tin and leave to stand at room temperature for 3 hours. Turn the marshmallow out onto a work surface dusted with the icing sugar mixture. Cut into squares and leave to dry for several hours. Dust with the remaining crushed amaretti biscuits.

Matcha is finely ground tea-leaf powder, traditionally used as part of the tea ceremony in Japan. Matcha adds a delicate flavour and pale green colour to these gourmet marshmallows. Because the tea is so finely powdered you can sprinkle some over the set marshmallows to decorate.

Japanese Matcha Marshmallows

- Makes 96 2.5cm/1in pieces

vegetable oil, for greasing
50g/2oz/½ cup icing
    (confectioners') sugar, for dusting
50g/2oz/½ cup cornflour
    (cornstarch), for dusting
2 large egg whites
400g/14oz/2 cups caster (superfine)
    sugar
15ml/1 tbsp liquid glucose or clear
    corn syrup
350ml/12fl oz/1½ cups cold water
60ml/4 tbsp powdered gelatine
50ml/2fl oz mandarin juice and
    finely grated rind of 1 large
    mandarin
10 Matcha green tea bags, or
    20g/¾ oz loose Match green tea
bamboo canapé sticks, to decorate

1 Prepare a 20cm x 30cm/ 8 x12in baking tin or pan at least 4cm/1½in deep following the instructions on page 14.

2 Whisk the egg whites until they form firm peaks (preferably using a stand mixer). Set aside.

3 Add the sugar, liquid glucose, and half of the water to a small pan and follow the method on page 14 until the syrup reaches the hard-ball stage (130°C/266°F).

4 Meanwhile, using the remaining water, prepare the gelatine following the method on page 15.

5 Add the mandarin juice to a measuring jug and top up with enough water to make 150ml/5 fl oz/ ²/₃ cup. Heat in a small pan until boiling. Add the Matcha tea bags to a small heated teapot, add the boiling liquid and leave to brew.

6 When the sugar syrup is ready, take it off the heat and carefully pour the dissolved gelatine into the syrup.

7 Turn the beater to full speed while pouring the hot syrup in a slow steady stream down the inside of the bowl. Continue to whisk until the marshmallow is stiff enough to hold its own shape. Turn the beater to a slower speed and gradually pour in the hot green tea. Add the mandarin zest and firmly squeeze by hand any remaining tea from the tea bags, into the marshmallow mixture.

8 Pour the mixture into the prepared tin and smooth it level. Leave to stand at room temperature for 3 hours.

9 Prepare the work surface, turn the marshmallow out and cut into squares as on page 16. Allow to dry for 2 hours and dust again. To serve, add a bamboo canapé stick to each and sprinkle with a little Matcha tea.

This recipe has all the flavours of the classic dessert. The sharp, clear fruitiness of raspberries, the scents of caramelized sugar from the crisply baked meringue, and the ultra creamy consistency of the mallow mixture. Utter indulgence for a summer's day picnic or al-fresco lunch.

Eton Mess Marshmallows

- Makes 96 2.5cm/1in pieces

vegetable oil, for greasing
50g/2oz/½ cup icing (confectioners') sugar, for dusting
50g/2oz/½ cup cornflour (cornstarch), for dusting
2 egg whites
400g/14oz/2 cups caster (superfine) sugar
15ml/1 tbsp liquid glucose or clear corn syrup
350ml/12fl oz/1½ cups cold water
60ml/4 tbsp powdered gelatine
30ml/2 tbsp lemon juice
115g/4oz raspberries, crushed very finely
4 small meringues, finely crushed
freeze-dried raspberries, or extra meringues very finely crushed to a powder, to decorate

1 Prepare a 20cm x 30cm/ 8 x12in baking tin or pan at least 4cm/1½in deep following the instructions on page 14.

2 Whisk the egg whites until they form firm peaks (preferably using a stand mixer). Set aside.

3 Combine the sugar, liquid glucose and half of the water in a small pan over a low heat and stir to dissolve the sugar. Bring to a steady boil and cook without stirring until the syrup reaches the hard-ball stage (130°C/266°F).

4 Meanwhile, with the remaining water, prepare the gelatine following the method on page 15.

5 When the sugar syrup is ready, take it off the heat and carefully add the liquefied gelatine (the mixture will bubble up in the pan). Stir in the lemon juice to combine.

6 Turn the beater to high speed while pouring in the hot syrup in a steady stream down the inside of the bowl until it is all combined, then continue to beat for 8–10 minutes, until the marshmallow mixture is stiff enough to hold its own shape.

7 Mix the crushed raspberries and meringue into the marshmallow mixture. Pour into the prepared tin and smooth it level. Leave to stand at room temperature for 3 hours.

8 Prepare the work surface, turn the marshmallow out and cut into squares as on page 16. Allow to dry out for 2 hours and dust again.

9 To serve, sprinkle the marshmallows with the freeze-dried raspberries, or using a sieve or strainer, dust with finely powdered meringue. Store in an airtight box layered with wax paper, or pack into small boxes to give as gifts.

Herbs can add a sweet subtle flavour to confectionery. Angelica adds a hint of aniseed and reduces acidity when it is cooked with rhubarb. Sweet cicely is a natural sweetener like angelica and will make a good substitute if angelica is not available: use the same quantity of leaves.

Rhubarb & Angelica Marshmallows

● Makes 35 4cm/1½in pieces

vegetable oil, for greasing
50g/2oz/½ cup icing (confectioners') sugar, for dusting
50g/2oz/½ cup cornflour (cornstarch), for dusting
175g/6oz young rhubarb (only use the red part of the stalks)
8 angelica leaves
30ml/2 tbsp caster (superfine) sugar
2.5ml/½ tsp powdered ginger
2 large egg whites
400g/14oz/2 cups caster (superfine) sugar
15ml/1 tbsp liquid glucose or clear corn syrup
350ml/12fl oz/1½ cups cold water
60ml/4 tbsp powdered gelatine
6 or 7 drops, or more, of dusky pink food colouring

1 Prepare a 20cm x 30cm/ 8 x12in baking tin or pan at least 4cm/1½in deep following the instructions on page 14.

2 Add the rhubarb and angelica leaves to a small pan with a lid, with 30ml/2 tbsp sugar, and enough water to barely cover the fruit. Poach gently for 5 minutes, remove the lid and cook for a further 6-7 minutes until the liquid has evaporated. Purée, then stir in the ginger powder and reserve 115g/4oz of fruit for the recipe.

3 Whisk the egg whites until they form firm peaks (preferably using a stand mixer). Set aside.

4 Add the caster sugar, liquid glucose, and half of the water to a small pan. Place the pan over a low heat and stir to dissolve the sugar. Bring to the boil and heat steadily until the syrup reaches the hard-ball stage (130°C/266°F).

5 Meanwhile, using the remaining water, prepare the gelatine following the method on page 15.

6 When the sugar syrup is ready, take it off the heat and carefully pour the dissolved gelatine into the syrup. Stir to combine.

7 Turn the beater to full speed while pouring the hot syrup in a thin, steady stream down the inside of the bowl, for about 4-5 minutes. Continue to whisk for a further 8-10 minutes with the food colouring added gradually in droplets to reach the desired colour.

8 Lightly work in the rhubarb purée (don't over-mix). Pour into the prepared tin and smooth it level. Leave to set for 3 hours.

9 Prepare the work surface, turn the marshmallow out and cut into flower shapes as on page 17. Allow to dry out for 2 hours and dust again.

Make sure to work the caramel finely into the marshmallow mix to form thin streaks. Thick streaks will create little pockets of caramel in the finished marshmallow, which may dribble down the sides of the small cut squares. Store them in the refrigerator in an airtight container layered between wax paper to firm up.

Salted Caramel Marshmallows

● Makes 96 2.5cm/1in pieces

vegetable oil, for greasing
50g/2oz/½ cup icing (confectioners') sugar, for dusting
50g/2oz/½ cup cornflour (cornstarch), for dusting
115g/4oz caster (superfine) sugar
25g/1oz butter
50ml/2fl oz ¼ cup double (heavy cream)
1.5ml/¼ tsp salt
2 large egg whites
400g/14oz golden caster (superfine) sugar
15ml/1 tbsp liquid glucose or clear corn syrup
350ml/12 fl oz/1½ cups cold water
60ml/4 tbsp powdered gelatine
10ml/2 tsp vanilla extract

1 Prepare a 20cm x 30cm/ 8 x12in baking tin or pan at least 4cm/1½in deep following the instructions on page 14.

2 Put the 115g/4oz caster sugar into a small pan and leave to melt over a medium to high heat, shaking the pan to distribute the sugar until it caramelizes evenly into a mid-amber colour. Stir in the butter, until it melts. Remove from the heat and stir the cream and salt well into the hot caramel. Stand over a pan of warm water to keep the caramel liquid.

3 Whisk the egg whites until they form firm peaks (preferably using a stand mixer). Set aside.

4 Add the 400g/14oz golden caster sugar, liquid glucose and half of the water to a small pan and follow the method on page 14 to turn the sugar syrup to a hard-ball stage (130°C/266°F).

5 Meanwhile, using the remaining water, prepare the gelatine following the method on page 15.

6 When the sugar syrup is ready, take it off the heat and pour the dissolved gelatine into the syrup. Stir to combine. Add the vanilla extract.

7 Continue to beat the egg whites while pouring the hot syrup in a slow steady stream down the inside of the bowl, and continue to whisk for a further 8–10 minutes until the marshmallow mixture is thick enough to hold its own shape while liquid enough to flow into the prepared tin.

8 Quickly mix in the cooled but still liquid caramel until the marshmallow has fine streaks. Immediately pour into the tin. Leave to set for 3 hours.

9 Prepare the work surface, turn the marshmallow out and cut into squares. Dry for 2 hours and dust.

These stylish cookies reveal a secret caramel centre oozing inside the piped vanilla 'fluff' marshmallow sandwiched between two Belgian galettes au beurre. They are truly delicious and special enough for a party. The galettes are readily available to buy in most large supermarkets.

Marshmallow Caramel Wafers

- Makes 20 wafers

40 Belgian galettes au beurre
2 large egg whites
400g/14oz/2 cups caster (superfine) sugar
15ml/1 tbsp liquid glucose or clear corn syrup
350ml/12fl oz/1½ cups cold water
60ml/4 tbsp powdered gelatine
20ml/4 tsp vanilla extract
105ml/7tbsp ready-made caramel

COOK'S TIP
Any leftover marshmallows may be piped into strips as a special sweet treat.

1 Prepare two large piping bags. Stand them upright inside tall measuring jugs or similar sized containers, and fold the tops of the bags over the rims of the containers to hold them steady.

2 Lay half the butter crisps onto a transferable work surface, preferably a large board.

3 Whisk the egg whites until they form firm peaks (ideally with a stander mixer). Set aside.

4 Add the sugar, liquid glucose, and half of the water to a small pan. Place over a low heat and stir to dissolve the sugar. Bring the mixture to the boil and continue to heat until the syrup reaches the hard-ball stage (130°C/266°F).

5 Meanwhile, using the remaining water, prepare the gelatine following the method on page 15.

6 When the sugar syrup is ready, take it off the heat and carefully pour the dissolved gelatine into the syrup. Combine with the vanilla extract.

7 Turn the beater to full speed while pouring the hot syrup in a slow, steady stream down the inside of the bowl. Continue beating for 8–10 minutes until the mixture is stiff enough to hold its shape, while thin enough to flow into the piping bags.

8 Transfer the marshmallow mixture into the two large pastry bags fitted with large 12 star nozzles. Pipe an oval circle of the marshmallow over the biscuits on the board, leaving a small 1cm/2in margin of biscuit around the edges and a little space in the centre, and add a spoonful of caramel to each.

9 Position and lightly press the remaining biscuits on top. Leave for several hours, until the mallow sets.

The chopped raisins soaked in rum add a warm taste sensation and harmonises well with the distinct flowery aroma of the vanilla-flavoured marshmallows. To serve, toast on clean, dry garden twigs, or metal skewers, until the marshmallows look golden and caramelized in parts.

Toasted Coconut Marshmallows

● Makes 96 2.5cm/1in pieces

vegetable oil, for greasing
50g/2oz/½ cup icing
  (confectioners') sugar, for dusting
50g/2oz/½ cup cornflour
  (cornstarch), for dusting
50g/2oz raisins, lightly chopped
30ml/2 tbsp rum (optional)
115g/4oz/1 cup sweetened
  desiccated (shredded) coconut
2 large egg whites
400g/14oz/2 cups caster
  (superfine) sugar
15ml/1 tbsp liquid glucose or clear
  corn syrup
350ml/12fl oz/1½ cups cold water
60ml/4 tbsp powdered gelatine
10ml/2 tsp vanilla extract

1   Prepare a 20cm x 30cm/ 8 x12in baking tin or pan at least 4cm/1½in deep following the instructions on page 14.

2   Add the chopped raisins to the rum (if using) and leave overnight. Preheat the oven 180°C/350°F/ Gas 4. Spread the coconut over a lightly oiled baking sheet. Cook, stirring occasionally, until it starts to brown. Transfer to the prepared tin and spread evenly over the base.

3   Whisk the egg whites until they form firm peaks (preferably using a stand mixer). Set aside.

4   Add the sugar, liquid glucose, and half of the water to a small pan set over a low heat and gently stir to dissolve the sugar. Bring the mixture gradually to a steady boil and continue to heat until the syrup reaches the hard-ball stage (130°C/266°F).

5   Meanwhile, using the remaining water, prepare the gelatine following the method on page 15.

6   When the sugar syrup is ready, take it off the heat and carefully add in the liquefied gelatine. Stir to combine.

7   Turn the beater to full speed while pouring in the hot syrup in a steady stream down the inside of the bowl until it is all combined. Add the vanilla extract and continue to beat for a further 8–10 minutes until the mixture is stiff enough to hold its own shape. Quickly fold in the chopped raisins and any rum juices.

8   Pour the mixture into the prepared tin and smooth it level over the toasted coconut. Set aside for 3 hours.

9   Prepare the work surface, turn the marshmallow out and cut into squares as on page 16. Allow to dry out for 2 hours and dust again.

This recipe makes a lovely neutral beige marshmallow with a marbleised pattern made by swirling the melted chocolate through the marshmallow mixture before it sets. Maya Gold chocolate is flavoured with orange and spices, but you can substitute another type of chocolate if you prefer.

Streaky Maya Chocolate & Vanilla

● Makes 96 2.5cm/1in pieces

vegetable oil, for greasing
50g/2oz/½ cup icing
  (confectioners') sugar, for dusting
50g/2oz/½ cup cornflour
  (cornstarch) for dusting
100g/3½oz Maya gold chocolate or
  an alternative dark (bittersweet)
  chocolate of your choosing
2 large egg whites
400g/14oz/2 cups golden caster
  (superfine) sugar
15ml/1 tbsp liquid glucose or clear
  corn syrup
350ml/12fl oz/1½ cups cold water
60ml/4 tbsp powdered gelatine
10ml/2 tsp vanilla bean paste
pinch salt

1 Prepare a 20cm x 30cm/ 8 x12in baking tin or pan at least 4cm/1½in deep following the instructions on page 14.

2 Place the chocolate in a medium heatproof bowl suspended over a saucepan of warm-hot water taken from the heat.

3 Whisk the egg whites until they form firm peaks (preferably using a stand mixer). Set aside.

4 Combine the sugar, liquid glucose and half of the water in a small- to medium-sized heavy pan set over a low heat and stir gently to dissolve the sugar. Bring the mixture gradually to a steady boil and cook without stirring until the syrup reaches the hard-ball stage (130°C/266°F).

5 Meanwhile, using the remaining water, prepare the gelatine following the method on page 15.

6 When the sugar syrup is ready, take it off the heat and carefully add the liquefied gelatine. Stir together. Add the vanilla bean paste and salt.

7 Continue to beat the egg whites while pouring the hot syrup in a thin steady stream down the inside of the bowl, for about 4–5 minutes until it is all combined. Continue to beat the marshmallow mixture until it is thick enough to hold its own shape while liquid enough to flow into the prepared tin.

8 Quickly mix in the cooled, slightly thickened liquid chocolate until the mixture has fine streaks. Pour into the prepared tin. Place in the refrigerator for 3 hours to set.

9 Prepare the work surface, turn the marshmallow out and cut into squares as on page 16. Allow to dry out for 2 hours and dust again.

Hokey Pokey is the Cornish term for honeycomb. You can make your own but it's easier to use store-bought chocolate-covered honeycomb bars. The fabulous texture, combined with the smooth milk chocolate, is a marriage made in heaven.

Hokey Pokey Marshmallows

● Makes 96 2.5cm/1in pieces

vegetable oil, for greasing
50g/2oz/½ cup icing
 (confectioners') sugar, for dusting
50g/2oz/½ cup cornflour
 (cornstarch), for dusting
2 large egg whites
400g/14oz golden caster (superfine)
 sugar
15ml/1 tbsp liquid glucose or clear
 corn syrup
350ml/12fl oz/1½ cups cold water
60ml/4 tbsp powdered gelatine
10ml/2 tsp vanilla extract
75g/3oz shop-bought chocolate
 honeycomb bars, crushed finely,
 plus extra, for dusting

1 Prepare a 20cm x 30cm/
8 x12in baking tin or pan at least
4cm/1½in deep following the
instructions on page 14.

2 Whisk the egg whites until they
form firm peaks (preferably using a
stand mixer). Set aside.

3 Add the sugar, liquid glucose and
half of the water to a small- to
medium-sized heavy pan. Place the
pan over a low heat and gently stir to
dissolve the sugar. Bring the mixture
gradually to the boil and continue to
heat steadily until the syrup reaches
the hard-ball stage (130°C/266°F).

4 Meanwhile, using the remaining
water, prepare the gelatine following
the method on page 15.

5 When the sugar syrup is ready,
take it off the heat and carefully pour
in the dissolved gelatine. Stir to
combine. Add the vanilla extract.

6 Continue to beat the egg whites at
full speed while pouring the hot syrup
in a thin steady stream down the
inside of the bowl, then continue to
whisk for a further 8–10 minutes until
the meringue is thick enough to hold
its own shape, while thin enough to
flow easily into the prepared tin.

7 Pour half the mixture into the
prepared tin and spread most of the
crushed honeycomb bars evenly over
the marshmallow, then top with the
remaining marshmallow and smooth
it with a palette knife. Leave to stand
at room temperature for 3 hours.

8 Dust the work surface with more
icing sugar and cornflour. Using a
palette knife, loosen the
marshmallow around the edges of
the tray and turn out onto the dusted
surface. Cut into pieces and lightly
dust with the remaining finely
crushed honeycomb. Leave to dry on
wire racks for several hours.

Choose a home-made or quality bought Seville orange marmalade which has a finely cut rind. The tangerine food colouring adds a pretty tint of orange, but do make sure to measure the droplets accurately or use a fine toothpick to gradually add colour paste or gel.

Seville Orange Marshmallows

● Makes 35 large marshmallows

vegetable oil, for greasing
50g/2oz/½ cup icing
　(confectioners') sugar, for dusting
50g/2oz/½ cup cornflour
　(cornstarch), for dusting
115g/4oz thin cut Seville
　marmalade
finely grated peel of 1 large orange
15ml/1 tbsp cognac
2 large egg whites
400g/14oz/2 cups caster (superfine)
　sugar
15ml/1 tbsp liquid glucose or clear
　corn syrup
175ml/6fl oz/¾ cup cold water
40ml/2½ tbsp lemon juice
60ml/4 tbsp powdered gelatine
approximately 14 drops tangerine
　food colouring or enough to add a
　delicate tint of orange to the
　marshmallows

1　Prepare a 20cm x 30cm/ 8 x12in baking tin or pan at least 4cm/1½in deep following the instructions on page 14.

2　Combine the marmalade, grated orange peel and cognac in a small pan.

3　Whisk the egg whites until they form firm peaks (preferably using a stand mixer). Set aside.

4　Add the sugar, liquid glucose and 175ml/6fl oz/¾ cup of the water to a small pan set over a low heat and cook until the syrup reaches the hard-ball stage (130°C/266°F).

5　Meanwhile, add the lemon juice to a measuring jug and top up with enough water to make 175ml/6fl oz/ ¾ cup liquid. Put in a bowl and sprinkle over the powdered gelatine. Leave to soak, then dissolve suspended over a pan of hot water taken from the heat.

6　Gently heat the marmalade and cognac mixture.

7　When the sugar syrup is ready, take it off the heat and pour the dissolved gelatine into the hot syrup. Stir to combine with the hot marmalade and cognac mixture.

8　Turn the beater to full speed while pouring the hot syrup in a steady stream down the inside of the bowl to combine, then continue to beat for about a further 8–10 minutes, gradually adding the food colouring in droplets, until the meringue looks pale orange and begins to thicken.

9　Pour the mixture into the prepared tin and smooth it level. Leave for 3 hours at room temperature to set.

10 Prepare the work surface, turn the marshmallow out and cut into squares or circles as on pages 16 to 17. Allow to dry out for 2 hours and dust again.

Chewy Nougats

Sweet, sticky and perfect for giving as a gift, or for a moment of pure indulgence, nougat can vary from a thick gooey torrone to a lighter, softer texture that melts in the mouth. Once you have mastered the basic method on page 18, try the following recipes, which feature cocoa and candied fruits and nuts to offer additional colour, flavour and crunch.

Nougat is made slightly differently in every country. This is an Italian version, which is weighted down to make it denser, but it is still gooey and light. The pure flavours of pistachio, honey and orange blossom marry beautifully, and the bright green pistachios look attractive when the nougat is cut.

Pistachio Nougat

• Makes about 1kg/2¼lb

grapeseed or groundnut (peanut) oil, for greasing
rice paper
375g/13oz/scant 2 cups caster (superfine) sugar
15ml/1 tbsp liquid glucose or clear corn syrup
100ml/3½fl oz/scant ½ cup water
120ml/4fl oz/½ cup honey
2 egg whites
250g/9oz/1½ cups whole almonds, lightly toasted and warmed
200g/7oz/1¼ cups pistachios, warmed
5ml/1 tsp orange blossom water

1 Grease a Swiss roll tin (jelly roll pan), then line with the rice paper.

2 Put 350g/12oz/1¾ cups of the sugar, the liquid glucose and water in a large, heavy-based pan and heat until it reaches the soft-crack stage (143°C/290°F).

3 Warm the honey in a separate pan until it just boils, then add to the syrup and bring everything up to 143°C/290°F again.

4 Meanwhile, whisk the egg whites with the remaining 25g/1oz/2 tbsp of the sugar until stiff peaks form.

5 Slowly pour the sugar and honey syrup into the whites in a steady stream, whisking constantly. Tiny lumps may form, but do not worry. Continue mixing until the mixture is stiff and glossy.

6 Add the toasted and warmed nuts and orange blossom water, and gently fold together. Pour the nougat into the tin.

7 Cover the mixture with more sheets of rice paper and weight down with a heavy board, such as a chopping board, and weights or dishes. If the chopping board smells strongly (of onions, for example), place something between it and the nougat or the nougat will take on the flavour. Leave to set for 4 hours.

8 Remove the weights and board, turn out on to a chopping board and trim the sides to neaten them. Slice into bars or squares and serve immediately, or store in an airtight container between layers of wax paper for 1 week.

Nougat can be a wonderful carrier for your favourite flavours. Here, the chewy egg white combines perfectly with the melty bits of chocolate, and is then finished off with the rice paper. If you want a more chocolatey version, these would also be delicious if cut into squares and dipped in tempered chocolate.

Cocoa Nougat

● Makes about 1kg/2¼lb

grapeseed or groundnut (peanut) oil, for greasing
rice paper
450g/1lb/2½ cups caster (superfine) sugar, plus 15g/½oz/ 1 tbsp
45ml/3 tbsp liquid glucose, or clear corn syrup
100ml/3½fl oz/scant ½ cup water
50g/2oz/½ cup unsweetened cocoa powder, plus extra for dusting
2 egg whites
200g/7oz/1¼ cups whole almonds, lightly toasted and warmed
100g/3¾oz dark (bittersweet) chocolate, finely chopped
5ml/1 tsp vanilla extract

1 Grease a Swiss roll tin (jelly roll pan), then line with the rice paper.

2 Put 450g/1lb/2½ cups of the caster sugar, the liquid glucose and water in a large, heavy-based pan and heat to the soft-crack stage (143°C/290°F).

3 Add the cocoa powder to the syrup and bring back to 143°C/290°F again.

4 Meanwhile, whisk the egg whites with the remaining 15g/½oz/1 tbsp of the sugar until stiff peaks form.

5 Slowly pour the syrup into the whites in a stream, whisking constantly. Tiny lumps may form, but do not worry. Continue mixing until the mixture is stiff and glossy.

6 Add the toasted and warmed nuts, chocolate pieces and vanilla and gently fold together. Pour the nougat into the prepared tin.

7 Cover the mixture with more sheets of rice paper and weigh down with a heavy board, such as a chopping board, and weights or dishes. Leave the nougat to set for 4 hours.

8 Remove the weights and board, and carefully turn out on to a chopping board. Lightly dust the top with cocoa powder and trim the sides to neaten them.

9 Slice into diamonds. Serve immediately, or store in an airtight container for about 1 week, with wax paper in between each layer.

There are two main types of nougat: white and brown. The white type is made with beaten egg whites and has a softer texture than the brown version, given here, which is made with caramelized sugar. It is a wonderful contrast in textures, with soft, chewy nougat studded with crisp nuts and sweet, candied fruit.

French Nougat with Candied Fruit

● Makes about 1.2kg/2½lb

grapeseed or groundnut (peanut) oil,
  for greasing
rice paper
375g/13oz/scant 2 cups caster
  (superfine) sugar
15ml/1 tbsp liquid glucose or clear
  corn syrup
100ml/3½fl oz/scant ½ cup water
350g/12oz/1½ cups honey
2 egg whites
300g/11oz good quality candied fruit
100g/3¾oz/½ cup whole almonds,
  toasted
75g/3oz/½ cup hazelnuts, toasted
75g/3oz/¾ cup flaked (sliced)
  almonds, toasted
75g/3oz/½ cup pistachios, warmed
2.5ml/½ tsp fresh or dried culinary
  lavender buds
pinch of salt
40g/1½oz/3 tbsp unsalted butter,
  cut into small pieces and softened

1 Grease a baking tray and line with rice paper, or grease a 15cm/6in square cake tin or pan and line with the rice paper for a thicker nougat.

2 Put 350g/12oz/1¾ cups of the caster sugar, the liquid glucose and water in a large, heavy-based pan, and heat to the soft-crack stage (143°C/290°F).

3 Warm the honey in a separate pan until it just boils, then add to the syrup and bring everything up to 143°C/290°F again.

4 Meanwhile, whisk the egg whites with the remaining 25g/1oz/2 tbsp of sugar until stiff peaks form.

5 Slowly pour the sugar and honey syrup into the whites in a stream, whisking constantly. Tiny lumps may form, but do not worry. Continue mixing until the mixture is stiff and glossy.

6 Chop one-third of the candied fruits and add to the mixture with the warm nuts, lavender buds and salt. Gently stir in. Add the butter and stir to combine.

7 Pour the nougat into the baking tray or tin and smooth the top level.

8 Decorate the surface with large pieces of the remaining candied fruits.

9 Leave to set at room temperature for 4–6 hours.

10 To remove the nougat from the tin, run an oiled paring knife around the edge and invert the cake tin, if using, or slip a metal offset spatula underneath the block if it is on a baking sheet.

11 Transfer to a chopping board and cut into small pieces and serve. Store in an airtight container for about 1 week. Do not refrigerate.

Index

This edition is published by
Lorenz Books, an imprint of
Anness Publishing Ltd
108 Great Russell Street
London WC1B 3NA

info@anness.com
www.annesspublishing.com

If you like the images in this book and would like
to investigate using them for publishing,
promotions or advertising, please visit our
website www.practicalpictures.com for more
information.

© Anness Publishing Ltd 2015

A CIP catalogue record for this book is available
from the British Library.

COOK'S NOTES

- Bracketed terms are intended for American readers.
- For all recipes, quantities are given in both metric and imperial measures and, where appropriate, in standard cups and spoons. Follow one set of measures, but not a mixture, because they are not interchangeable.
- Standard spoon and cup measures are level. 1 tsp = 5ml, 1 tbsp = 15ml, 1 cup = 250ml/8fl oz.
- Australian standard tablespoons are 20ml. Australian readers should use 3 tsp in place of 1 tbsp for measuring small quantities.
- American pints are 16fl oz/2 cups. American readers should use 20fl oz/2.5 cups in place of 1 pint when measuring liquids.
- Electric oven temperatures in this book are for conventional ovens. When using a fan oven, the temperature will probably need to be reduced by about 10–20°C/20–40°F. Since ovens vary, you should check with your manufacturer's instruction book for guidance.
- The nutritional analysis given for each recipe, unless otherwise stated, is calculated for the whole recipe.
- Large (US extra large) eggs are used unless otherwise stated.

PUBLISHER'S NOTE

Although the advice and information in this book are believed to be accurate and true at the time of going to press, neither the authors nor the publisher can accept any legal responsibility or liability for any errors or omissions that may have been made nor for any inaccuracies nor for any loss, harm or injury that comes about from following instructions or advice in this book.

Publisher: Joanna Lorenz
Editor: Helen Sudell
Photographer: Nicki Dowey
Food Stylist: Annie Rigg, Claire Ptak
Prop Stylist: Wei Tang
Designer: Lisa Tai
Production Controller: Pirong Wang

NUTRITIONAL NOTES

Vanilla Marshmallows Energy 2224kcal/9481kJ; Protein 59g; Carbohydrate 529g, of which sugars 476.3g; Fat 0.3g, of which saturates 0.1g; Cholesterol 0mg; Calcium 250mg; Fibre 0.1g; Sodium 197mg

Peppermint Marshmallows Energy 2382kcal/10165kJ; Protein 9g; Carbohydrate 625g, of which sugars 566g; Fat 0g, of which saturates 0g; Cholesterol 0mg; Calcium 56mg; Fibre 0g; Sodium 144mg

Raspberry Heart Marshmallows Energy 2274kcal/9699kJ; Protein 61.8g; Carbohydrate 538.2g, of which sugars 485.5g; Fat 0.9g, of which saturates 0.3g; Cholesterol 0mg; Calcium 300mg; Fibre 5g; Sodium 203mg

Marshmallow Sticks Energy 2224kcal/9481kJ; Protein 59g; Carbohydrate 529g, of which sugars 476.3g; Fat 0.3g, of which saturates 0.1g; Cholesterol 0mg; Calcium 250mg; Fibre 0.1g; Sodium 197mg

Rose Water Marshmallows Energy 2382kcal/10165kJ; Protein 9g; Carbohydrate 625g, of which sugars 566g; Fat 0g, of which saturates 0g; Cholesterol 0mg; Calcium 56mg; Fibre 0g; Sodium 144mg

Blueberry Marshmallows Energy 2541kcal/10813kJ; Protein 59.4g; Carbohydrate 610.3g, of which sugars 551.2g; Fat 0.7g, of which saturates 0.1g; Cholesterol 0mg; Calcium 346mg; Fibre 4.3g; Sodium 407mg

Lemon Sherbet U.F.O.'s 3116kcal/13278kJ; Protein 60.3g; Carbohydrate 754.6g, of which sugars 681.3g; Fat 4.8g, of which saturates 1.4g; Cholesterol 19mg; Calcium 363mg; Fibre 0.1g; Sodium 2343mg

Angel Marshmallow Cornets Energy 3141kcal/13382kJ; Protein 106g; Carbohydrate 706g, of which sugars 586.8g; Fat 7.6g, of which saturates 3.8g; Cholesterol 0mg; Calcium 544mg; Fibre 1.7g; Sodium 703mg

Fluffernutter Lollipops 2876kcal/12105kJ; Protein 49.3g; Carbohydrate 451.2g, of which sugars 357.7g; Fat 109.4g, of which saturates 30.5g; Cholesterol 67mg; Calcium 279mg; Fibre 0g; Sodium 677mg

Rocky Road Marshmallow Pops Energy 196kcal/821kJ; Protein 2g; Carbohydrate 26g, of which sugars 22g; Fat 10g, of which saturates 6g; Cholesterol 14mg; Calcium 27mg; Fibre 0.3g; Sodium 62mg

Pina Colada Marshmallow Swirls Energy 186kcal/794kJ; Protein 1g; Carbohydrate 47g, of which sugars 47g; Fat 0g, of which saturates 0g; Cholesterol 0mg; Calcium 11mg; Fibre 0g; Sodium 23mg

Apricot & Amaretti Marshmallows Energy 2550kcal/10869kJ; Protein 64.6g; Carbohydrate 593.9g, of which sugars 519g; Fat 7.2g, of which saturates 3.1g; Cholesterol 0mg; Calcium 396mg; Fibre 8g; Sodium 566mg

Japanese Matcha Marshmallows Energy 2241kcal/9556kJ; Protein 58.9g; Carbohydrate 533.6g, of which sugars 480.3g; Fat 0.4g, of which saturates 0.1g; Cholesterol 0mg; Calcium 284mg; Fibre 0.1g; Sodium 399mg

Eton Mess Marshmallows Energy 2320kcal/9897kJ; Protein 61.3g; Carbohydrate 551.7g, of which sugars 498.5g; Fat 0.7g, of which saturates 0.2g; Cholesterol 0mg; Calcium 310mg; Fibre 3.9g; Sodium 418mg

Rhubarb & Angelica Marshmallows Energy 2235kcal/9535kJ; Protein 60.3g; Carbohydrate 530.6g, of which sugars 477.3g; Fat 0.5g, of which saturates 0g; Cholesterol 0mg; Calcium 442mg; Fibre 3.3g; Sodium 399mg.

Salted Caramel Marshmallows Energy 2924kcal/12433kJ; Protein 60.1g; Carbohydrate 650.2g, of which sugars 597g; Fat 27.2g, of which saturates 16.7g; Cholesterol 69mg; Calcium 337mg; Fibre 0.1g; Sodium 1000mg

Marshmallow Caramel Wafers 3713kcal/15705kJ; Protein 35.3g; Carbohydrate 716.6g, of which sugars 572.3g; Fat 98.4g, of which saturates 27g; Cholesterol 188mg; Calcium 542mg; Fibre 6.7g; Sodium 1015mg

Toasted Coconut Marshmallows Energy 2829kcal/11997kJ; Protein 63.4g; Carbohydrate 568.1g, of which sugars 514.8g; Fat 42g, of which saturates 36.1g; Cholesterol 0mg; Calcium 317mg; Fibre 12.6g; Sodium 444mg

Streaky Maya Chocolate & Vanilla Energy 2733kcal/11616kJ; Protein 63.7g; Carbohydrate 592.7g, of which sugars 538.5g; Fat 28.4g, of which saturates 16.9g; Cholesterol 6mg; Calcium 312mg; Fibre 3.4g; Sodium 400mg

Hokey Pokey Marshmallows Energy 2597kcal/11047kJ; Protein 65.2g; Carbohydrate 572.7g, of which sugars 510.1g; Fat 20.9g, of which saturates 10.1g; Cholesterol 8mg; Calcium 376mg; Fibre 3.9g; Sodium 514mg

Seville Orange Marshmallows (per individual marshmallow) Energy 28kcal/119kJ; Protein 1.6g; Carbohydrate 5.5g, of which sugars 3.9g; Fat 0g, of which saturates 0g; Cholesterol 0mg; Calcium 6mg; Fibre 0g; Sodium 13mg.

Pistachio Nougat Energy 4838kcal/20294kJ; Protein 103.3g; Carbohydrate 577.8g, of which sugars 554.5g; Fat 251.1g, of which saturates 21.1g; Cholesterol 0mg; Calcium 1293mg; Fibre 33.3g; Sodium 264mg

Cocoa Nougat Energy 3893kcal/16394kJ; Protein 62g; Carbohydrate 611g, of which sugars 570g; Fat 150g, of which saturates 32g; Cholesterol 6mg; Calcium 631mg; Fibre 26g; Sodium 751mg

French Nougat with Candied Fruits Energy 5644kcal/23755kJ; Protein 62.8g; Carbohydrate 878.1g, of which sugars 859.8g; Fat 233.4g, of which saturates 36.8g; Cholesterol 92mg; Calcium 1171mg; Fibre 36.4g; Sodium 1388mg